D0264509

Books should be returned on or before the
last date stamped below

14. JUL. 08

09. SEP. 09
19. MAY 09

19 AUG 2010

20 JUL 2011

3 JAN 2013
(HQ)

10 SEP 2014

26 NOV 2014

20 AUG 2016
05 SEP 2017

17 SEP 2019

A L I S

1592375

Other titles in this series

Dyslexia and Maths
Julie Kay and Dorian Yeo
1-85346-965-3

Dyslexia and English
Elizabeth Turner and Jayne Pughe
1-85346-967-X

Dyslexia and Physical Education
Madeleine Portwood
1-85346-970-X

Dyslexia and Modern Foreign Languages
Gaining Success in an Inclusive Context
Margaret Crombie and Elke Schneider
1-85346-966-1

Dyslexia and Drama

Helen Eadon

 David Fulton Publishers

David Fulton Publishers Ltd
The Chiswick Centre, 414 Chiswick High Road, London W4 5TF

www.fultonpublishers.co.uk

David Fulton Publishers is a division of Granada Learning, part of
ITV plc.

First published 2005
10 9 8 7 6 5 4 3 2 1

British Library Cataloguing in Publication Data
A Catalogue record for this book is available from the British
Library.

ISBN 1 84312 048 8

Eadon, Helen

Dyslexia and
drama / Helen
Eadon
                371.
                9144
1592375

Typeset by GCS Composing Services, Leighton Buzzard
Printed and bound in Great Britain by Ashford Colour Press.

Contents

Acknowledgements

I would like to thank the following persons and organisations for their help and support:

Gillian Chatterton
The British Dyspraxia Foundation
Dr Sionah Lannen
The students of the Red Rose School
Dr Gavin Reid

Foreword

It is a privilege to write the foreword for this book. We are confident that it will be warmly welcomed by all teachers; speech and drama specialists in particular will appreciate it. It will be relevant for teachers in both primary and secondary schools. To an extent, all teachers, particularly in primary schools, engage in speech and drama activities. Such activities are fun and motivating. This book has a comprehensive chapter outlining these types of activities, flavoured by the author's own personal and professional experiences.

Dyslexia is an area that is still clouded in controversy and confusion. This is not helpful for the class teacher who often recognises the talents in children but is perplexed as to why some children may not be making the expected progress in some subjects. This, of course, could be due to dyslexia, or to some other specific learning difficulty. In this book Helen Eadon provides a succinct outline of dyslexia and the other associated difficulties that students may experience. She describes the characteristics of dyslexia and the implications they have for teaching drama.

There is also an insightful chapter on children's own experiences. This is an important chapter because children need to be heard, particularly children with dyslexia. They may be harbouring strong emotional feelings of frustration and, in some cases, anger. Helen reiterates throughout this book the importance of self-esteem for learning and for life. There is also a chapter focusing on the needs and views of parents. This is an important issue because communication with parents is vital. It is important to ensure that the links between home and school are constructive.

There is an emphasis here on both the child and the curriculum. The book contains a plethora of strategies and information to help teachers deal with dyslexia effectively, and we congratulate the author on her work.

Dr Lindsay Peer CBE
Dr Gavin Reid

Chapter 1

Dyslexia

What is dyslexia?

Dyslexia affects around 10 per cent of the population. This means that in virtually every class it is likely that there will be at least one person with the disorder. The British Dyslexia Association defines dyslexia as a difference in the area of the brain that deals with language. Brain imaging techniques show that dyslexic people process information differently. This difference in processing affects the underlying skills that are needed for learning to read, write and spell.

Dyslexia, however, affects more than reading or writing; it can have an impact on learning, memory and organisation. The 'popular' view of dyslexia is that it is a condition that affects reading and writing. This is understandable as the word 'dyslexia' comes from the Greek meaning 'difficulty with words'. It is important, however, to be aware of the range of characteristics associated with dyslexia. These will be discussed throughout this book. It is also important to be aware of the individual differences, the needs and the learning preferences of students with dyslexia.

Characteristics of dyslexia

The main characteristics of dyslexia are:

- lack of fluency and speed in reading
- hesitant predictive reading (using context)
- hesitancy in reading

- losing the place in reading
- failing to recognise words
- low level of comprehension
- difficulty using dictionaries

Students with dyslexia will usually have difficulty with reading and this can include any or all of the above. Difficulties in reading comprehension may be due to a lack of understanding but could be attributed to weakness with reading fluency. Additionally, if the student is light-sensitive or colour-sensitive, a suitably coloured overlay or tinted glasses may help.

Writing

The problems associated with writing are as follows:

- poor handwriting
- badly set out work
- lack of punctuation and grammar
- difficulty copying from the board or from a book

Dyslexic students can be frustrated when it comes to writing. Often there is a block with the transfer of ideas from their imagination to the blank exercise book in front of them. Handwriting may lack style and consistency, as may grammar and punctuation. These problems will be heightened under stress, particularly in exams and tests. Spelling difficulties are an obvious problem and can be a source of frustration.

Self-esteem

Reading and writing aside, one of the most significant difficulties faced by the dyslexic student is lack of self-esteem and confidence, which is probably the most acute problem when it comes to drama.

The first day at secondary school is a big step to take. Suddenly the student finds him/herself in an unfamiliar building, with new teachers and a range of different subjects. For all students these factors can cause stress, but for most it would only be temporary. The dyslexic student will also have difficulties in reading, spelling, writing and possibly mathematics, and these factors will contribute to low self-esteem.

We all have a self-image and we develop strategies to deal with our own imperfections, but if we begin to believe that we are inadequate, then eventually we will behave as if this were true. Undermining a child by destroying their self-esteem will have a significant effect on their potential to learn and on their success in life. Dyslexic children need to feel supported in order to succeed.

It is common in secondary schools that the differences between dyslexic students and others become apparent in learning and in basic attainments. At first there may only be slight discrepancies, but if new skills are taught to the dyslexic learner without effective strategies to accompany them, then he/she will fail and a low self-esteem will result. The dyslexic child will probably be the first to realise that there is something wrong, and may not discuss his/her worries with parents or teachers. This is a vicious cycle that may lead to emotional and personal difficulties.

In order for learning to be successful, the student must value him/herself as well as others. Dyslexic learners entering secondary school will have already faced failure, so secondary schools must be aware of the needs and problems that they are bringing with them.

Achieving in drama

All of these difficulties could stand in the way of potential achievement in drama.

If we look at the area of reading first, we can see that a difficulty could cause problems with script work. In this case, when introducing a new script or play to the group, it might be best to summarise the whole plot first, before a full read-through. The next step would involve preparing improvisations around the main characters and storylines. This would mean that the students would have a general idea of the play before they start to read. It may be possible for the play or script to be transferred to an audio device so that the student can follow the words while hearing someone else read them. It may be traumatic for the dyslexic student to be given the script in black-and-white format, especially if they have scotopic sensitivity which involves visual acuity. It may be helpful to photocopy the script onto coloured paper and make the font bigger.

In a situation like this the role of a Special Support Assistant (SSA) would be valuable; if there are a few students with a learning difficulty, the assistant could work with the group on the content of the script, going over unfamiliar words and making the lines familiar to the students, thus saving the embarrassment of having to sightread in front of the whole class.

Of course, there are times when reading aloud is necessary. If the student normally uses his/her finger to follow the words, try suggesting the thumb technique. I use this technique with all my students, dyslexic or otherwise. Hold the script with both hands and make sure that you have a thumb on each page. As you start to read down the lines, your thumb moves with you, so even if you look away, your thumb will indicate which line you are on.

Correct posture is important for all students, and it may be worthwhile devoting a lesson to this and reinforcing it from time to time. When we are nervous or tense we hunch up, making breathing and speaking more problematic. By using correct breathing and positive techniques, students will feel more relaxed and in control and will undoubtedly give a better performance. This, of course, will lead to better self-confidence.

The teacher must make it clear what is expected from the students and must be ready to repeat instructions as necessary. This way, the student will be confident of knowing what to do. It should be made clear that they are working in a safe and protected environment. With the right approach the drama lesson will engender in the students a sense of achievement, regardless of their academic ability.

Group games build trust among individuals and these activities should be accessible to all. It would be best to start off with easier games and then progress to harder ones as time goes on. (See 'drama ideas' in Chapter 3 for suggested games.)

It is important that both teacher and student see progress in the work. This can be achieved through assessment techniques. A drama diary can be kept by the students, where they can record their own progress and keep a checklist of targets. The SSA could help individuals record their thoughts and feelings, even by mind mapping® (see Chapter 3).

Writing frames

Writing frames might be produced by the teacher to assist self-analysis. These would include the following headings:

Topic

Title

Outline of idea

Best part of my performance

In future I would change...

I could improve by...

Similarly styled frames may be useful when writing play reviews. Again, mind-mapping techniques can be used, instead of general note-taking, when watching a performance. The mind map would give a plan and a starting point for writing up the review.

Suggestions

You will have your own rules to which the students should adhere. However, keep in mind the following:

- Always warm up and cool down with appropriate activities (cooling-down games are very important – it is difficult, as we all know, to teach a sit-down, formal lesson to a group of students who are buzzing from a physical drama lesson).
- Encourage *all* students to exercise self-discipline.
- Give as much praise and feedback as you can – all students thrive on encouragement and develop self-confidence – not just dyslexic ones.
- Ensure that everyone knows the rules of the activity – repeat them to reinforce them.
- Don't interfere too much – let imagination and creativity lead the way.

Explanations of and responses to dyslexia as a syndrome

Theoretical background – conflicting perspectives

The different perspectives of those working in the field of dyslexia have been described as an 'ecosystem' by Rod Nicolson at the fifth BDA conference. He described those working in dyslexia research as 'a group with overlapping but often conflicting needs attempting to inhabit the same space'. Quite often, the viewpoints of researchers involved in the area of dyslexia will be conflicting, stating differences in approaches rather than shared common ground. These different perspectives on dyslexia can be confusing for teachers.

However, there has been progress in dyslexia research involving new techniques in neurosciences, brain-imaging and genetics. These theories have been classified by Frith (1995, 2002) on three levels: biological; cognitive; and behavioural.

Nicolson and Fawcett (1999) suggested that the cerebeller deficit hypothesis was an important factor in dyslexia. It had been known for some time that the cerebellum is involved in speed-learning and motor skills, and further research suggested that it might also be involved in language dexterity. Again, on a psychological level, the work of Galaburda (1993) had an influence both in the conceptual understanding of dyslexia and in practice. His work suggested that dyslexic adults and children may prefer to use right-hemisphere skills when learning. This may have implications for subjects such as drama.

Right-hemisphere processing relates to tasks that require a holistic approach – seeing the whole picture. On the other hand, left-hemisphere processing involves analysis of detail and small chunks of information. West (1997) used this information to emphasise the positive side of dyslexia, saying that right-hemisphere people can often have an advantage. This is pertinent to drama, as creativity involves right-hemisphere skills but the learning of words is essentially a left-hemisphere task.

Phonological aspects

At a cognitive level, the dominant theory in dyslexia has been the phonological deficit hypothesis. This theory has been supported by considerable research (Bradley and Bryant, 1991; Hatcher and Snowling, 2002). This suggests that learning to read is an interactive process that involves the use of different language skills. Hatcher and Snowling state that activities such as non-word reading are problematic because of the difficulties associated with sound symbol relationships. This is seen as one of the most robust signs of dyslexia. The evidence for this view comes from studies, some of which investigate the development of dyslexic children before they fail to read. This was done by following children who were at a higher risk of being dyslexic, e.g. if they (a) had dyslexic parents and (b) had difficulties with early language skills and activities such as rhyming.

Wolf and O'Brien (2001) have suggested that dyslexia can be described as a 'double-deficit hypothesis'. This means that in addition to phonological differences, dyslexic children have a processing speed difficulty and therefore process information more slowly.

Fawcett (2002) comments that children with dyslexia 'show impairments in a wider range of skills, including sensory deficit (flicker, motion sensitivity, rapid auditory discrimination), motor (bead threading, balancing) and cognitive (phonological, working memory, speed)'. She noted that there seemed to be a difference in the 'fluency' with which dyslexic pupils carried out the tests.

This hypothesis, known as Dyslexia Automaticity Deficit (DAD), was suggested to highlight the difficulties children with dyslexia may have with automaticity of learning. The research found that when children were asked to perform two tasks simultaneously, dyslexic children experienced problems with balancing in particular and had difficulty in completing the tasks.

Dyslexia as a syndrome

Nicolson (1996) suggested that 'for many years there has been considerable unease as to how developmental dyslexia should be defined'. This relates to distinguishing dyslexia from poor reading. Nicolson and Siegel (1996) suggested that although people display dyslexia in different ways, and there are sub-types of dyslexia, dyslexia is a syndrome. This view has been challenged by some researchers such as Stanovich (1996) who argues that research has failed to find any qualitative difference in the performances of dyslexics and poor readers.

In response to this notion of dyslexia as a syndrome, and how the syndrome can be precisely defined, there are a number of different views from researchers working in the field. One view is that of Stanovich; he questions the assumption whether poor readers of high or low intelligence need different explanations for their reading difficulties. This fits with Frith's belief that reading difficulties may not necessarily be a product of dyslexia, and that the problems could be social-emotional, of environmental origin, and that by improving the teacher–pupil relationship, reading and writing skills might improve. Stanovich believes that intelligence has nothing to do with reading ability and that the problem lies within the 'word recognition module', including the reading of pseudo-words, phonological segmental language skills, orthographic processing and spelling–sound regularity, whether of high or low intelligence. He questions why a child with a low IQ, speech problems, poor phonological skills, poor word recognition skills and poor comprehension skills may not be dyslexic.

Tunmer and Chapman (1996) have an important view that should be considered in the teaching of dyslexic children. They argue that dyslexia is the result of a meta-cognitive dysfunction affecting the phonological processing model, despite utilising correct environmental and linguistic opportunities. This means that children acquire and use inefficient cognitive strategies to deal with reading. As a result of these repeated learning failures, dyslexic children will have a low expectation of themselves and a low self-esteem. They must therefore be made aware 'that they can achieve by using more effective learning strategies'.

In opposition to Stanovich, Nicolson believes that IQ is important to the dyslexia theory. He believes that the phonological deficit hypothesis is not a complete account of the difficulties that dyslexic children encounter. He also says that we must distinguish between poor readers with a low IQ from those who are dyslexic, in order to differentiate the cause of phonological deficits. Nicolson goes on to suggest that early identification should lead to proper support, which should avoid reading problems in the future.

Snowling (1998, 2000) believes that characteristic features of dyslexia are independent of intelligence and relate to phonological processing. She feels that if sensitive enough testing is used then phonological difficulties will be found. She goes on to argue that dyslexia is a form of language impairment affecting the phonological features of spoken words encoded in the brain, as a result of poorly specified phonological representations. In addition to this, Snowling says that dyslexia affects the development of reading and spelling skills. However, its effect can be changed through appropriate use of developmental skills.

Conclusion

It is quite clear that there is still controversy as to how dyslexia can be defined. We must realise that dyslexia is a label and that everyone placed in that category is an individual with their own strengths and weaknesses regardless of intelligence or reading ability. It could be argued that tests are not necessarily as valid as they should be. In my own experience, I have worked with children who have overcome reading difficulties and are able to read a book aloud, yet when tested in reading isolated words their reading score is lower than the standard of books they are capable of reading. This is because they are capable of predicting words when they form part of a sentence, but when words are singled out they find it harder. This has been noted by Reid (2003) who explains that 'bottom-up/top-down' approaches to reading suggest that fluent readers look first at the component features of the letters in words before they consider the meaning of the actual word. Top-down readers, on the other hand, anticipate the meaning of the text before checking for syntax and graphical clues. Stanovich backs this theory up by suggesting that some children are more dependent on visual clues while others rely on contextual ones. Again this shows how each child is different, relying on their own individual ways of encoding and processing information.

Chapter 2

Dyslexia and Drama

This chapter focuses on the drama curriculum and those features within it that may have an influence on children with dyslexia.

Stage KS3/GCSE

Drama is a very important lesson on its own or as a cross-curricular activity. It enables students to:

- understand themselves and others
- develop literacy skills
- develop teamwork and communication
- self-educate
- problem-solve and make decisions
- build self-esteem and confidence
- explore issues and experiences in a safe and supportive environment
- follow rules

All of the above skills are vital for all students, but are especially important for the dyslexic learner.

Drama makes up an important part of English. It stands alongside reading and writing and makes up a separate strand of speaking and listening at Key Stage 3. It becomes a subject in its own right at GCSE.

The National Curriculum details drama objectives as follows. Each student should:

- identify with characters and actions through role-play (e.g. in a dramatised story and as spectators of a performance);
- have the confidence and ability to put across a particular point of view;
- learn how to work with others to solve human and practical problems;
- create and take part in improvised scenes in order to explore issues;
- invent and develop convincing roles in specific situations;
- know how to structure dramatic sequences in order to convey meaning;
- be aware of the need for dramatic conventions (e.g. light, dark, movement, pause, sound, silence);
- be aware of and use a variety of dramatic forms and techniques to express ideas and feelings (e.g. mime, movement, costume, make-up, props, set design);
- appreciate drama in performance, both as participants and as spectators;
- understand the educational, cultural and social purposes of drama;
- develop a vocabulary of theatre/drama;
- explore the variety of human emotions through drama;
- learn to listen and concentrate;
- learn to respect and, where appropriate, depend on others (e.g. trust skills);
- develop awareness (sensitivity) and enjoyment of the ways groups work (e.g. decision-making, problem-solving, negotiation, willingness to accept responsibility, a democratic approach);
- evaluate achievements as an individual and through groups and learn critical awareness;
- appreciate the values and attitudes of own and others' communities, recognise social conventions and stereotypes and be prepared to examine them;
- explore cross-curricular themes.

Drama requires a clear sense of discipline and direction from both teachers and students. All are equally responsible for the quality of learning that takes place.

Exam criteria

Assessment objectives

The GCSE Drama and Theatre Arts syllabus will assess the candidate's ability to:

- demonstrate knowledge and understanding of practical skills and techniques relevant to Drama and Theatre Arts;
- respond imaginatively and relevantly to a given stimulus in a dramatic context;
- demonstrate practical skills and techniques associated with Drama and Theatre Arts;
- evaluate work carried out in studies relating to Drama and Theatre Arts.

Scheme of assessment

- coursework (60%)
- controlled test (40%)

The table below shows the weighting of the assessment objectives.

Objective	Controlled test	Practical coursework	Written
Knowledge and understanding of practical skills and techniques		10%	10%
Imagination and relevant response to a given stimulus	10%	10%	
Demonstration of practical skills and techniques	30%	20%	
Students' evaluation of their own work			10%
Total	**40%**	**40%**	**20%**

There are external exams that are available in the field of drama. These include those given by the London Academy of Music and Dramatic Arts, which have recently been accredited. For the purposes of this book we will be focusing on the GCSE syllabus and its accessibility to the dyslexic student.

Coursework (60%)

Two of the following options, only **one** of which may be a technical/design skill:

1. Devised thematic work for performance to an audience
2. Acting
3. Theatre in education presentation
4. Improvisation
5. Dance/drama
6. Set
7. Costume
8. Make-up
9. Properties
10. Masks
11. Puppets
12. Lighting
13. Sound
14. Stage management

Each option is assessed through 50% practical work (preparatory work and end-product) and 10% response to the process of development. Internally assessed and externally moderated.

Written paper (40%) – 2 hours

A choice of any **two** questions based on the following sections:

A. Set plays – a choice from six
B. Response to live productions seen during the course

Externally set and marked.

At a glance the scheme of assessment (60 per cent coursework and 40 per cent written paper) could work well for the dyslexic student. However, a two-hour literacy based exam may seem daunting and might deter candidates from taking the GCSE if they were not given the appropriate help and support.

The Joint Council for General Qualifications gives an explanation of the rationale for special arrangements in its Regulations and Guidance (JCGQ 2001).

The awarding bodies recognise that there are some candidates who have coped with the learning demands on a course but for whom the standard arrangements for the assessment of their attainment may present a barrier. Such barriers may arise as a result of:

- a permanent or long-term disability or learning difficulty;
- a temporary disability, illness or indisposition;
- English being a second or additional language; or
- the immediate circumstances of the assessment.

Inclusion and special arrangements

The SEN and Disability in Education Act 2001 (SENDA 2001) applies to all UK education provision and ensures that schools and colleges consider minorities in all assessments. The Inclusion Statement of the English National Curriculum states the following:

Overcoming Potential Barriers to Learning and Assessment for Individuals and Groups of Pupils

- Teachers must take account of these requirements and make provision, where necessary, to support individuals or groups of pupils to enable them to participate effectively in the curriculum and assessment activities. During end of key stage assessments, teachers should bear in mind that special arrangements are available to support individual pupils with disabilities.

- Not all pupils with disabilities will necessarily have special educational needs. Many pupils with disabilities learn alongside their peers with little need for additional resources beyond the aids, which they use as part of their daily life, such as a wheelchair, a hearing aid or equipment to aid vision. Teachers must take action, however, in their planning to ensure that these pupils are enabled to participate as fully and effectively as possible within the National Curriculum and the statutory assessment arrangements. Potential areas or difficulties should be identified and addressed at the outset of work, without recourse to the formal provisions for disapplication.

- Teachers should take specific action to enable the effective participation of pupils with disabilities by planning appropriate amounts of time to allow for the satisfactory completion of tasks.

It is interesting to note that special arrangements for tests and assessments at key stages remain simple; GCSE special arrangements are less straightforward. Due to the rise in the 1990s of applicants, developments in national policy and SEN procedures, changes were brought about. Where regulations permit schools to make a decision – for example extra time or rest breaks – an educational psychologist or specialist teacher can write a report specifying individual needs. A history of provision can validate a request for special arrangements. With a decision held by the awarding body, again a specialist teacher and/or educational psychologist will write a report detailing the candidate's assessment needs. A history of individual needs and provision made for these needs must be included.

Subject content

The GCSE Drama coursework component states that 'Candidates must offer two different options for coursework', and that 'there is also a requirement for GCSE specifications in Drama that all candidates must present some performance work'. Candidates may therefore present only one technical and design skill option for assessment.

Group 1 – Scripted work

Devised thematic work for performance to an audience:

Acting
Set
Costume
Make-up
Properties
Masks
Puppets
Lighting
Sound
Stage Management

Work for the technical and design skill options must contribute to a group performance of scripted work.

Group 2 – Unscripted work

Devised thematic work for performance to an audience:

Improvisation
Theatre in Education presentation
Dance/drama
Set
Costume
Make-up
Properties
Masks
Puppets
Lighting
Sound
Stage Management

Work of the technical and design skill options must contribute to a group performance of unscripted work.

It is important that all students make informed choices of their specialist areas and that they are not merely told what to do. It is the general assumption of many that dyslexic students are naturally creative. This is not always the case, as Peer (2001) points out: 'some children have outstanding creative skills, others have strong oral skills, yet others have no outstanding talents'.

The coursework component of the GCSE should pose no great hindrance to the dyslexic student (if appropriate help and guidance are given, as mentioned previously); however, the written paper might.

Written paper

The written paper assesses all Assessment Objectives and comprises two sections:

A. Set plays
B. Response to live productions seen during the course.

Candidates may choose either section or both. Consideration should be given to the following aspects as necessary:

*   Characterisation
*   Voice – volume, accent, pace, timing, emotional range
*   Physical qualities – movement, posture, gesture, facial expression
*   Visual qualities – costume, make-up, properties

- Design qualities – scale, shape, colour, texture
- Use of scenic devices, lighting and sound
- Social context and genre
- Awareness of health and safety factors

Candidates should study their chosen set texts from a practical perspective and from the viewpoint of their preferred area of either performance or design. Candidates would find it helpful to have had practical experience of applying their chosen area either in workshop presentations or in full productions of their chosen set play(s).

In preparing for the examination, and in their answers, candidates should be aware of the potential effectiveness for an audience. They should be able to demonstrate their understanding of practical skills (AO1), their knowledge and understanding of the chosen play from a performance perspective (AO2) and analysis and evaluation of the effectiveness of their ideas (AO3). They should also be aware of the social context and genre of the play (AO2).

Candidates will be offered a choice of six questions, one on each of the set plays. Within each question candidates will be offered an alternative of either a performance or design perspective from which to approach their answer.

Candidates are expected to take **plain** copies of the chosen play(s) into the examination.

The plays set for the examination in 2004, 2005 and 2006 are as follows:

Brecht: *The Caucasian Chalk Circle*
Foxton: *Sepia and Song*
Miller: *The Crucible*
Potter: *Blue Remembered Hills*
Shakespeare: *Twelfth Night*
Waterhouse and Hall: *Billy Liar*

Set texts will be unchanged up to and including the 2006 examination. Thereafter there will be changes of one or two texts each year, which will be published annually in the Spring term and posted on the website.

Candidates are required to review a production of live professional or non-professional theatre that they have seen. Productions chosen must be of scripted plays; they must be substantial, complete texts, as defined in Section 8.3. Candidates are required to have studied the text before or after seeing the production and to be able to demonstrate their knowledge and understanding of the text.

Candidates should be able to demonstrate:

- a clear understanding of the play and the production;
- informed criticism of the acting performances and the skills involved;
- their response to the technical and design elements and the skills involved;
- their response to the effectiveness of the production as a whole.

Candidates may take personal notes relating to the production(s) into the examination.

Requirements for access to texts and to personal notes on live productions

There are QCA requirements for access to texts, which apply to GCSE Drama as follows:

- Plain texts must be used. Annotation is not permissible.
- Details of the edition used in the examination room must be provided. The rubric for Section A therefore requires candidates to give these details at the start of their answers.

In relation to the second point, teachers should ensure that candidates are aware, in advance of the examination, of the details to be provided. The name of the publisher is required, accompanied by Student Edition or Acting Edition if applicable.

- The notes of each production must not exceed two sides of A4 and must be in note form, not continuous prose, nor must they be in essay or theatre form.
- The notes must be the candidate's personal notes. Any printed material, e.g. programmes from a theatre visit, teachers' notes or notes marked or annotated by teachers are prohibited.
- The notes may be handwritten or word-processed.
- The personal notes will be collected at the end of the examination and will be sent to the examiner with the scripts. The notes will not be returned to centres and will therefore need to be photocopied if required in the future.

We are reminded that for the written paper a choice of any two questions based on the following sections must be answered by the candidate:

A. Set plays – a choice from six
B. Response to live productions seen during the course

In my opinion I would advise preparing to answer questions for section B. As stated earlier, the printed version of the plays for section A can be overwhelming and confusing for the dyslexic student whereas personal notes can be taken into the exam for section B. The requirements state that 'the notes may be handwritten or word-processed'. It does not state that colour or diagrams cannot be used, therefore a mind map on the performances might be an acceptable form of note-taking for the exam. The candidate would have prepared the notes themselves and would therefore be familiar with the layout and content.

Summary

The Drama GCSE curriculum is accessible to the dyslexic student. Full access to the drama curriculum would help with other curriculum subjects, as the course aims to encourage candidates to develop:

• an understanding of and response to a wide range of play texts, an appreciation of the ways in which playwrights achieve their effects and the ability to communicate the authors' intentions to an audience;
• an awareness of social, historical and cultural contexts and influences through an investigation of plays and other styles of dramatic presentation;
• increased self- and group awareness and the ability to appreciate and evaluate the work of others.

These aims would help to promote skills of creativity, self-confidence, concentration, self-discipline and communication. Drama, therefore, can be a useful resource to help the student with dyslexia overcome some of the academic and self-esteem hurdles that are often, for them, the reality of the learning experience in both primary and secondary school.

Chapter 3

Examples from Practice

Preparation for lessons
Mind mapping®

'While traditional learning such as taking notes used very few of the brain's resources, Mind Maps® encompass all the skills, combining logic, words, colour and pictures.'
Phillip Chambers, World Mind-Mapping Champion

The term 'mind mapping'® was first used in 1974 by Tony Buzan in his book and the BBC television series *Use Your Head.* However, it has taken some time for it to be accepted in education.

The method of mind mapping uses the whole brain, with a bias towards the right brain, 'whole picture' thinking process. It is highly visual and uses key words and pictures to recall information. Different colours and symbols can also be used, making it an ideal technique for dyslexic students. Mind mapping can be used by teachers and students alike.

Because of the high success that dyslexic students have in producing work using mind mapping, it has actually been incorporated into the timetable at the school where I work. I use it mainly in literacy lessons, but it can be used across the curriculum and, as stated earlier, would be of use in GCSE drama. Instead of the more usual note-taking, students could mind map performance reviews, which would later stimulate the memory and aid them in writing.

Mind mapping can be done freehand or by using one of the many computer software packages now available. If free-handing the mind map you must always start with a blank canvas, be it a sheet of paper or a whiteboard, starting in the centre with the topic you are mapping. Use different colours, draw lines coming away from the centre and use block capitals to write your main ideas on each strand. Secondary ideas can then be drawn off each main strand and you can use small-case letters, pictures or symbols to represent these ideas. You can add or take away as your map becomes more detailed.

Mind mapping is used within the Red Rose School, both freehand and by using software. The program 'Mind Genius' by Gael Ltd is used mainly. Originally it was developed for business use but now has many applications for educational work. Tony Buzan says that 'Mind Genius makes excellent use of mind mapping techniques, not only preparing students for the needs of education, but also for employment and indeed life'. Buzan lists the benefits of mind maps:

- They automatically inspire interest in the students thus making them more receptive and co-operative in the classroom.
- They make lessons and presentations more spontaneous, creative and enjoyable, both for the students and the teacher.
- They enable teachers' notes to become less rigid, more flexible and adaptable. In these times of rapid change the teacher needs to be able to alter and add to teaching notes quickly and easily.
- They present only relevant material in a clear and memorable form, enabling students to get better marks in examinations.
- They show not just the facts but also the relationship between those facts, thus giving the students a deeper understanding of the subject.
- They enable the volume of lecture notes to be reduced dramatically.
- They are especially useful for children with learning difficulties, particularly dyslexia. By freeing the child from the 'tyranny of semantics', the mind map allows the child a far more natural, complex and accelerated expression.

Reflective learning

Colour and light

Reflective learning can be split into two components: conditions; and reflections on own thought and behaviour. The first component is extremely important when dealing with the dyslexic student and the classroom. It has been shown that lighting, sound and furniture design can all have an impact on learning. Some children like the blinds up and the lights on, others prefer the main light off and the blinds part way down. Each child has their own preference so they have their choice of working conditions. Bright light can cause unrest and disruption among some children, yet others are unaffected. Dunn *et al.* (1985) believe that lighting can either increase or decrease academic achievement for many students who react strongly to the intensity of light.

An observation was carried out by Barbara Given, a learning styles consultant. She saw how the power of lighting could affect behaviour. When the light in the classroom was bright and strong, the majority of the students' facial expressions tightened, their eyelids drooped and they put their heads on the desk, while the teacher's behaviour continued as normal. After the lighting had been changed, i.e. blinds lowered, lights off, the behaviour of the children changed; they became more willing to co-operate. However, the teacher's behaviour also changed from a light-hearted to a more serious manner.

The colour of classrooms can also have an effect on learning and behaviour. At the Red Rose School the Educational Psychologist carefully selects colour schemes for different rooms to create the desired mood effect.

Sound is another important part of the learning environment and, again, its power should be used to full advantage.

Music

Don Campbell (2001) writing in *The Mozart Effect* believes that some sounds have healing and restorative powers and can enhance concentration and academic performance. Other sounds interfere with learning, even for those who prefer background sound. He writes that:

> Sound is energy that can be organised into shapes, patterns, figures and mathematical proportions, as well as into music, speech and utterances of agony and bliss ... We absorb these energies and they subtly alter our breath, pulse, blood pressure, muscle tension, skin temperature and other internal rhythms.

In the school we play Mozart concertos as they have a calm and energising effect. The same music is also played in hospitals for premature babies and burns patients and in recovery rooms, as it can promote rapid healing.

When using sound in school we must realise that although some students like sound, others do not. Perhaps students who respond well to sound could be allowed to use Walkmans playing appropriate music.

Ideas for drama

As a drama teacher there are goals that you have to reach and sometimes it can be difficult to find resources for activities to reach those goals. A lot of drama game books are aimed at younger children and play scripts for older children tend to have too many parts or characters. The London Academy of Music and Dramatic Art have good resources for solo work and for small groups. Their books are published by Oberon.

On the Internet there is a list of games and activities written especially for Key Stage 3 and GCSE Drama. They have been adapted by Simone Hennigan of South Hunsley School in the East Riding of Yorkshire. I hope that you enjoy these games. Some of them you may know, others may be new.

Freeze-frame

Introducing freeze-frame
Move away from your chairs and find a space. The teacher says [adapt this as necessary]: 'In a minute I want you to get into the group size I call out and form a snapshot from our imaginary album. [Use the list you have made on the flipchart paper and adapt it, e.g. in fours – a holiday snap; in sixes – a party; whole class – a football match or a community celebration.] I will count from ten to one and then say "Hold it and freeze." Hold the picture you have made until I say "relax".'

Go through about ten freeze-frames, quickly making comments on any good ones you see. If there are any which particularly impress you by their clear depictions, body language, facial expressions and so on, ask the rest of the class to relax and look at them and discuss the strengths of each one.

Tableaux to create simple improvisations from freeze-frames
Begin by asking the class to form simple freeze-frames in small groups, e.g. typical photo album snaps. Ask the whole class to produce two large-scale freeze-frames of first day at school and end of term (facial expressions are important). Split the class into two large groups – A and B. Ask each group to create a photo freeze-frame from the members of the other group. Give each group until the count of ten to mould the opposite group into the picture. Give the finished product a title. From the enforced picture each group must produce two minutes' worth of improvisation, either before or after the freeze.

Role play
Introduce the activity with these words, or a variation to suit your own situation:

Go back to your chairs. In groups of four, talk about a memorable event that happened during the holidays. If nothing interesting happened to you, invent something! Decide on a freeze-frame to start the drama. You are going to bring it to life for 30 seconds and use words this time. You have three minutes to practise it. The events can be quite commonplace, like going shopping with friends, or extraordinary, like witnessing an accident.

After two minutes stop the class and tell them that they have one minute left to work on their best moment in the drama. During this time you must move about the class, helping, questioning and encouraging the students. Your job is to motivate at this early stage. Keeping the student under pressure of time helps to clarify and focus the role play, otherwise it can ramble.

Now you are ready to bring the freeze-frames to life. Get the students to relax and ask for volunteers to show their freeze-frames and role play to the class.

Ask each group to hold their freeze-frame and then count down: '3, 2, 1, GO!' After about 30 seconds say: 'And freeze'.

Respect for their peers is essential. Take a bit of time with this. Try and find something good in each group, but do not tolerate walking off. It will spoil the drama in the long run if the students do not take their work seriously. Do not tolerate chatting while others are showing their work. They are practising their audience as well as performance skills.

Extending the role play

Introduce the activity with these words, or a variation to suit your own situation:

Get into groups of four. One of you works for a local paper or TV company, in a seaside town that is very short of news at the moment. Your job is to go to the beach and interview tourists. The rest of the group are the tourists. All of you need to spend one or two minutes deciding what makes a newsworthy item. Practise this for five minutes, deciding what makes a start with a freeze-frame, and be ready to bring it to life for 30 seconds. Set this up as before (with preparation time of two minutes).

See all the groups. Praise everything you can, but point out things that are obviously wrong and see if the group can identify what would improve it. As their confidence grows, gradually introduce more detailed and constructive criticism.

You are looking for examples of realism, controversy, humour and inventive treatment of the situation.

Mime

Walking with beasts

In this mime, pupils become creatures in an alien or prehistoric environment. They can do this individually, or several can join to form one large animal. Ask them to contort themselves and make their faces ugly, scary or unusual. You will talk them through a series of activities:

It is night – they must stay still, so predators cannot see them, but they may make occasional strange noises, as they sleep and dream.

Gradually, light begins to grow as the day breaks. Creatures stir and wake. Now, fully awake, animals may move around, mark territory or look for food. Animals may attack or prey on one another.

It begins to rain. Creatures find a place to shelter. They explore environment, find a mate and so on.

Tableaux and movement

Do this in groups of four or five. Each group has three titles:

The Feather is Falling
Moving the Piano
Stretch that Jumper

Encourage the pupils to think laterally and to produce frozen movements which are original. Avoid the obvious. They should link each picture with movement, counting the steps. Everyone should be in time and synchronised. Think about arms as well as legs and facial movements.

Improvisation
Titles for spontaneous improvisations
Use titles from this list to inspire or challenge students:

Quick change	Excuses	Wanted: Trainee
No Smoking	Pardon me, but could you...?	
Change in status	Waiting Room	
Help!	Stuck	
Keep off the grass	Engaged	

Scenarios for improvisation
These are ideas for scenarios with two performers – so students should work in pairs (or threes) with one directing. The situations work best if the pupils get straight into them and avoid long discussions.

Director instructing rather useless, awkward, overpaid actor
Fortuneteller and client
Hairdresser and customer (after hair disaster)
Photographer and awkward supermodel
Traffic warden and driver about to get a ticket
Married couple watching TV – arguments over what to watch
Casualty – nurse informing family of bad news
Two tramps arguing over box/newspaper/bench
Two strangers on a train – one lights up in a non-smoking compartment
Suspect being interviewed by the police
Boss giving employee the sack
Door-to-door salesman and lonely pensioner

Pregnant woman and claustrophobic stuck in a lift
Job interview
Parent and teenager – teenager three hours late, parent waiting up
Two cars meet coming from opposite directions down a narrow country
lane. One belongs to farmer, the other to a wealthy businessman –
who moves?
Boyfriend proposing to girlfriend – she's trying to dump him
Pupil sent to head for bad behaviour
Doctor and patient – patient is a hypochondriac
Two wrestlers warming up, or two men on the moon

Prop boxes
Students prepare spontaneous (no time for prior discussion or
preparation) or polished improvisations in groups of two, three or
more using objects in prop boxes as stimuli (can be made up of any
object, e.g. hat/book/ball).

Titles from teacher
The Letter
Good News
Get Your Hair Cut
The Doctor and the Patient
Frou-Frou the Wonder Dog, or The Dog that Can Do Amazing Tricks
Crime
The Eavesdropper
The Baby
The Girl with Green Hair
Kidnapped
Gangsters
Marooned on a Desert Island
The Green Paper Bag
In the Middle of the Night
A Fairy Tale
Family Matters
The Secret Formula
The Box of Chemicals
The Key
The Door Marked 'Private'
Fire
The Hijacker

In the Aeroplane
The Time Machine
The Secret
Grandad
Beauty and the Beast
The Dream
The Man from the Council
Mother and Son
Father and Son
The Boy (or Girl) Who Wouldn't Speak
Old Uncle Bayram
The Thieves
Danger at the Zoo
The American Girl
Robbery with Violence
The Stranger at the Door
The Doctor
The Forbidden Planet
The Bomb that Wasn't
The Birthday Surprise
The Conflict
Robots
Bad News
The Bully at the Bus Stop
Shock
Gunman City
The Visitor who Came to Tea
Rat Poison
In the Year 2100
Planet X
Accident
The Black Box
The Special Dress
Incident at the Bus Stop
The Nagging Mother
The Monster
Ebenezer Scrooge
The Hat
Dial M for Murder
Two Workmen

The Haunted House
Whodunnit?
World War II
The Gipsy Fortune Teller
The Nightmare
Grandma
Spoilt Children
The Truants
Teacher's Pet
Mother and Daughter
Father and Daughter
I Can Read Your Thoughts
Pauline and the Pop Star
Divorce
The Invisible Mane
Baby-snatcher
Poison Gas
The Man-Eating Plane
Grandad's Will
Please Don't Tease
Round the Flats
The Telephone
Money, Money, Money
It's Just Not Fair
Why Don't You Ever Listen to Me?
My Dog's Just Died
What's the Big Idea Then?
Go On, Amaze Me!
You've been talking about me behind my back, haven't you?
I saw you hit my little brother
Don't go on and on about it
Please don't tell her I told you
What ever possessed you to do it?
You jealous or something?
He's/she's packed me in
Why do you tell so many lies?
That's an excellent piece of work, but there's just one thing…
You've just been chosen for a mission from which you are very unlikely to return
I don't want to go to school today

How can I tell him/her that it's over?
Do you know something? You really get up my nose
Why are you always in such a bad temper?
Why did you tell Mum on me?
Dad's mad with you
Don't be such a greedy-guts
Stop pretending to be something you are not!
Don't be a dog in the manger!
Why can't you ever see it from my point of view?
Why did you hurt Mum's feelings like that?
You've got things out of all proportion
Mum said never accept lifts from strangers
What a waste of money!
How dare you treat your pet like that?
I told you before, you must not bunk off school
You're all mouth and no trousers
It's easy to be an armchair critic – don't just sit there, do something!
Why do you give up so easily?
Haven't you got any manners?
Get up out of that bed immediately!
If you don't mind my saying so, you need to go on a diet
I hate to say this, but I think you've got anorexia nervosa
Look, I'm only giving you a warning

Eventually, students should be in a position to use skills acquired and their own imaginations to create group improvisations lasting between three and five minutes. If you wish to impose a more rigid structure consider:

- three-scene performances for all improvisations;
- freeze-frames at beginning and end of a performance and possibly of each scene too;
- a checklist of techniques, for example one scene must be mime or involve talking to the audience.

Starters and fill-ups
Use starters for warming up before a session. Fill-ups are useful activities to fill in extra time.

Sometimes warm-up games are useful for starting a session. They can raise the energy level of a group, calm down a boisterous one and improve concentration and focus. They can also be used at the end of a session as a way of bringing a class back together, or simply when you have a spare ten minutes at the end of a session and it is not worth starting new work.

You may wish to use some of the frames and exercises to help students improve their skills in improvisation, observation, listening or inventiveness, for example. If so, make the aim of the exercise clear to the class, as an overdose of seemingly pointless game-playing is demotivating for students in the long run. Try to keep a balance between fun and serious activities.

In this section there are frames for the whole class (warm-ups and calm-downs) and also starting points for small group work.

The class are seated in a circle
One person is chosen to mime holding a cardboard box, placing it on the floor in front of them and opening the lid to take out an imaginary object. The person then handles or uses the object for a moment before placing it back in the box.

The rest of the group are then invited to put their hands up if they think they can guess what the object is. The person who guesses correctly can then open the next box and the game begins again.

As a variation on this, or if the imaginary object is hard to guess, it may be passed around the circle. The leader may give clues as to its identity by making comments such as 'Be careful, it can bite' or 'Mind, it's slippery/cold/wet/sticky', etc.

Name that person
This game is very useful for getting to know a new class. The activity becomes tedious with a group larger than 20 but it is a surprisingly effective way for a teacher to learn new names or for a group to get to know one another.

The class stands in a circle and everyone says their name in turn. One person is chosen to start. This pupil must look at someone in the circle and call that person's name. Once it has been called, the caller walks to the other person's place.

Meanwhile the person whose name has been called must look at a third person, call that person's name and walk towards her/him. No-one must leave his or her place before calling the name of the person whose place they intend to take. Make sure that everyone moves at least once during the game.

What are you doing?
This game is good for energising a group and freeing the imagination. It also requires concentration and develops skills in mime.

The group stand in a circle. One person begins to mime an activity – for example, mowing the lawn or posting a letter.

The person next to him/her asks 'What are you doing?' and the first person is obliged to say something different from what he/she is actually doing (e.g. 'I'm frying an egg'). The second person must then mime the first person's answer until the third person asks 'What are you doing?', at which point he/she must make up another lie for the third person to act out.

This game can go round the circle twice before you stop it – unless the students are particularly inventive!

Lines and proverbs
Groups of three to six students can be given the following lines or proverbs as the theme for a short improvisation. The lines need not actually be spoken. The improvisation can simply reflect the subject matter.

Lines
I knew it would end like this.
It's not my fault.
Why don't you get a job like the others?
I'm sorry, I didn't mean it.
No-one here understands me; I may as well leave.
Have you heard the latest?
This is nothing to do with me; I'm staying out of it.

Proverbs
A rolling stone gathers no moss.
A friend in need is a friend indeed.
Too many cooks spoil the broth.
Handsome is as handsome does.
A bird in the hand is worth two in the bush.
A stitch in time saves nine.
Absence makes the heart grow fonder.

Group shapes
This is a simple game but it needs co-operation. Ask students to walk around the room using all the space and trying not to bump into each other. Once this is established, call out a shape which the whole class must form. Start with a circle as this is easy. Other useful shapes include: triangle; square; diamond; any capital letter; five-pointed star; umbrella.

The whole class must make one shape between them, as though it were to be viewed from the air. Between making shapes, ask them to walk steadily as before, using all the space in the room.

Drama and media – advertising campaign
(preparation work / warm-ups / the advertising agency / the advertising campaign)

Preparation work
Display: pupils produce advertisement collages where they examine different advertising styles/techniques (such as before and after, celebrity endorsement, comparison, humour, pseudo-science, narratives, etc.).

Warm-ups
Verbal: any quick-fire word games, such as Word Tennis
Physical: mirror-imaging, hand hypnosis
Improvisation: give each pair a prop and allow them 30 seconds to prepare an advertisement. Perform to the group, swap props and repeat

Variation: create another use of the prop (e.g. a hairbrush becomes a mobile phone) and act it out.

Shake hands or introductions

Pupils have one minute to shake hands with everyone in the room and ask for four bits of information:

- favourite colour
- favourite food
- home town or village
- birthday

After one minute, get everyone seated and see what they can remember about each other.

Name circles

Sit in a circle and introduce yourself, then ask the child on your right to introduce himself/herself, plus you. The next child on the right then has to introduce himself/herself, plus the previous child, plus you, and so on until it comes back to you. The last child will have to introduce everyone in the group! This can be done as a group activity with everyone reciting the list as it grows.

Jumping name circle

Stand in a circle and get everyone to do a star jump while shouting their own name. Then choose a starting point in the circle. Everyone must count to three, then jump. At the same time, the student who has been chosen to start shouts his or her name. On the second jump everyone else repeats that student's name. Keep up the rhythm as you work around the rest of the group, jumping and repeating names.

Co-operation circle
Form a circle, then sit down with feet and legs straight. Take hold of the hands (or wrists) of the people on either side of you. The object is to stand up without bending your knees or letting go of your partners. The winners are the ones who realise that you must help others before you can help yourself!

Sitting circle
Begin standing quite close together, then all turn to the right and on the command 'Go!' try to sit on the knees of the person behind you! If it works, everyone is supporting someone else, so the weight is evenly distributed.

Gesture circle/follow my leader
All sit in a circle and choose one person to lead (the teacher could start, to give an example). Whatever the leader does (movement or gesture) the rest must follow. Now choose someone to be the 'detective'. This pupil must leave the room while you choose the leader. They then re-enter the circle and try to determine who's in charge of the movements. Remind them that if everyone stares at the leader, it will be obvious – they must devise another way around it.

Wink murder
The 'detective' leaves the room while you choose a 'murderer' (either in front of other students or ask them to close their eyes and tap the murderer on the back). The detective enters the circle and the murderer can begin winking at his or her victims, who must try to die convincingly. The detective has three chances to identify the murderer – if he/she fails, the murderer must then reveal himself or herself. Being the murderer yourself makes an interesting variation!

Squeezing circle
All must hold hands in a circle (or wrists if they prefer). Choose one to begin sending a 'squeeze' message around the circle, by squeezing others' hands or wrists (you can vary the number of squeezes and speed rhythm). Now choose one to be the 'detective'. This student must enter the circle (after you have secretly chosen the student to begin the message) and try to identify who has the squeeze. To make it more difficult, choose more than one to begin the message.

Group count
The players have to count to twenty. They must only speak one at a time, and are not allowed to pre-plan the sequence. If two people say the same number, or if there is a gap (as judged by the teacher), the game starts again.

Impossible knots
In a circle the group hold hands and do not let go. Someone is nominated as a lead person and begins to weave in and out of the others, going under and stepping over other people's hands. When sufficiently knotted, the group has to unravel itself back into the original circle without speaking.

Summary

This chapter has provided examples that can be used in improvisation and within the scheme of work in a formal curriculum framework. Drama is one of the few subjects that has almost a free licence in this respect. Activities can be improvised and made to be fun, yet at the same time the student is developing crucial skills in learning and social development. This is ideal for the student with dyslexia as it makes learning fun and motivating. Furthermore, it is possible that by using some of the strategies highlighted in this chapter the student with dyslexia can experience success. This can have considerable implications for self-esteem and performance in other curriculum areas.

Chapter 4

Children's Views and Experiences

There is no substitute for experience. Experiencing the feelings and the views of children with dyslexia is important in order to gain a fuller understanding of the challenges they face in learning. All dyslexic children are different – they are individuals. It is important to recognise their individuality.

It is important that teachers understand the difficulties that these students have faced and will face, and, more importantly, how they deal with them. It is disheartening when students with dyslexia are not identified or fully assessed. This can lead to low self-esteem, failure and frustration, which, in turn, may lead to disruptive behaviour.

Below are some examples of dyslexic children's written thoughts, feelings and coping strategies.

Anthony

My mum thought I was dyslexic when I was two years old. When I was doing a jigsaw I was slower than my brothers. I found out in Year 5. I was ten. In Years 1 to 5 I got picked on. In Year 6 my class built up my confidence. I found out when I was watching TV with a dyslexic film on. I asked my mum 'Am I dyslexic?' She said 'yes'. I said 'cool'.

My teacher in Class 3 in Red Rose School helps me a lot. She understands me. Drama helped me a lot with my co-ordination.

Daniel

At my previous schools I had trouble with everything – reading, writing, spelling and maths. Other people called me names and made fun of my running. I had lots of tests with my brain. I found out I was dyslexic but I didn't understand what that meant. At Red Rose School what has helped me most is everyone understanding me and being patient.

David

At my previous schools things were terrible. I was bullied and picked on because I was always behind with my work. I found out I was dyslexic through my mum's friend who knew about dyslexia and I had a test. I was pleased to find out what my problems were because I knew it wasn't just me and I had an answer so I could get better. This school has boosted my confidence. Drama lessons have brought me 'out of my shell'.

Adam

When I was not at Red Rose School I got beaten up so I would want to go home so much I would try to go home by running away from school.

Richard

Before I came to Red Rose School I was told I had dyslexia. I was always behind with my work. I got bullied by a boy at school. When I found out I was relieved. What helped me most was coming to the Red Rose School. I am more confident.

Jordan

After moving from two different schools my mum said that you have to go for a test because we think you are dyslexic, so I went and I found out that I was dyslexic. I carried on struggling and then my mum found me a special school to go to. I am still at the Red Rose School and it is the best school.

Chris

I was in Year 1 when I found out that I was dyslexic. My teacher said that it would be okay. I had some tests and then my behaviour went from bad to worse. My teacher sent me out but I did not know why or what I had done wrong. I used to be sent to the head teacher because

I had not finished my work. It was always the same. I also got picked on by some people in my class. At the beginning of Year 6 we had a test to see what group we would go into and I passed by two marks just to get into the bottom group. Life was miserable and my self-esteem used to be low.

Tom (A)

I was 10 when I found out I was dyslexic. I knew that something was wrong but I didn't understand what was wrong. Now, looking back on this, some of the hardest times of my life were not knowing what was wrong with me and trying to do the same work as everyone else but finding it even harder to do.

I have a lot of anger inside of me. The reason why is because people thought I was not trying to do well, but I was. I was trying even harder than the rest of the class at this time. I was often seen in my class crying over my work. Just looking at it made me cry, and sometimes now it makes me cry inside when there is something I find hard to do.

The other kids in the classroom made fun of me too. I was crying as I could not do the work. I also found it hard to get on with some teachers and they had a go at me too for not trying. I was trying to learn but finding it a lot harder to learn, and it is still hard to talk about what happened to me. I still get scared inside when I find something hard but I'm learning to get over this problem.

Tom (B)

When I found out I was dyslexic I was about five years old and I was pretty annoyed. I thought I was thick at my old school. I used to get bullied but then I moved to Red Rose School. It is a lot better and I get a lot more help there. The teachers are great.

Drama has helped me talk in front of people because I never used to have confidence, but Mrs Eadon has helped me a lot. I have become a lot more expressive. I would like to thank my mum and dad and my family and the Red Rose School.

P.S. People who are dyslexic, just ask for help!!!

Lisa

Before I found out I was dyslexic, I went to high school. I was always falling behind with my work and the teachers gave me more homework than others did. Most of the time I didn't understand it. I didn't get any help either, so I got detention for it.

I was always getting bullied every day. The teachers did nothing about it and if they did, it ended up worse than before!

When I found out I was dyslexic it did come as a relief to me because I wasn't thick, and dyslexia was the reason that I was falling behind with my work and probably being bullied as well.

My best friend is dyslexic, and before I found out she thought that I should take the test. When I found out she helped me with the work at school and we worked together, helping each other. We still do. My family has been great and has supported and helped me.

I ended up moving to a special school. When I got there I was pleased. Since I got there I have not been bullied and I have made lots of friends. The teachers understand me, and you can bond with them. They help you whenever you are stuck or don't understand something. You don't feel left out.

Drama gives me confidence, helps my self-esteem and gives me valuable social skills which will be useful in years to come. As well as this, drama games can help with my dyspraxia, which is vital.

Jade

I found that I was a bit strange to other people. I could cope with the work, though I got bullied by a girl. I went to high school and the work seemed OK, but that was because it was only the first week. I felt I was a bit left out of the group that I was hanging around with. I didn't want to go to school. When I found out that I was dyslexic it wasn't a big surprise. I thought that I had it. I just tried to carry on as normal. My friends and family helped me by being nice and understanding. When I came to Red Rose and settled in I loved it. The small classes are great. The teachers can concentrate more on a one to one basis. Friends are great and everyone is friends with everyone else and knows what it is like. I feel better and more confident. I feel that my social skills have improved and I can mix more. Drama helps me with co-ordination and self-esteem, also social skills. I like drama a lot.

Lawrence

I couldn't do my work, I was always behind with it and being sent out of the classroom. I was bullied by other kids and nothing made any difference. I felt like the whole world was against me. When I found out that I was dyslexic I tried to carry on as normal, but it was not possible. I moved to a special school and I felt better. The classes were smaller and everyone was dyslexic. I was relaxed and NOT LEFT OUT!

My mum and dad helped me the most. My mum tried to get me a statement and I got one, and I also got a support teacher to help me. This September I am integrating back into mainstream high school.

Richard

I felt I was left out and I couldn't do my work. I was always behind in my work. Other kids bullied me and no-one seemed to do anything about it. I had no friends and I felt bad. When I found out I was dyslexic I understood why I was bullied at school and the teachers treated me differently. I did have a helper but they helped the rest of the class instead of just me. My family moved me to a special school. When I got there I felt better and I was more confident and relaxed. My social skills developed and the teachers understood. Drama gives me more confidence and helps with my social skills.

Comment

These accounts from children with dyslexia highlight very clearly the challenges and traumas they face. They also indicate how sensitive children with dyslexia can be when faced with an uncomfortable learning situation. For many, a large school can be an uncomfortable environment as there is a tendency for them to become 'lost' or 'forgotten'. Relationships and a feeling of belonging are important, and in a large school this may be more difficult to achieve. Yet the reality of the situation is that most secondary schools and many primary schools are large, and therefore pose additional challenges and threats to the emotional development and stability of children with dyslexia.

School size, however, is not the only important factor. One theme that came out very strongly in the above accounts was the sense of being taken seriously (or not) and that teachers need to make an effort to acknowledge and understand dyslexia. Children with dyslexia often have a good personal understanding of their strengths and weaknesses, but they still need the teacher's help in enabling them to believe in themselves. When their dyslexia is not fully diagnosed or supported they can feel confused and perplexed. This in itself can lead to low self-esteem, as in Tom Benson's account, when he says:

I knew that something was wrong but I didn't understand what was wrong. Now, looking back on this, some of the hardest times of my life were not knowing what was wrong with me and trying to do the same work as everyone else but finding it even harder to do. I have a lot of anger inside of me.

Feelings of frustration are very common for children with dyslexia and can lead to anger and subsequent behavioural difficulties in the classroom. The frustration can arise when they know they have abilities but are not able to display those abilities in their classroom performance.

One of the reasons for a chapter such as this is to ensure that the voices of children with dyslexia are heard and that their views and feelings are understood. Without this the development work on the curriculum, the differentiation of tasks and the selection of appropriate resources will not have as powerful an impact as they should.

Perhaps it may be suggested that the starting point for classroom planning should not be the curriculum or the syndrome of difficulties the students experience but the learners themselves – their views, their feelings and their aspirations.

Jay

*Peering through the looking
   glass
You see your own reflection,
But no one knows the person
   inside
You hide for your own
   protection.*

*I used to feel so lonely
In that tunnel away from
   the rest,
But now I am getting some
   more help
I can only do my best.*

*People who don't understand
They sometimes pity me,
No-one knows that hurt inside
   of me
Only my mum and I can see.*

*The light is getting brighter
My futures looking good,
For now there's people to help
So I am not misunderstood*

*So looking back at my reflection
I can see my inside
For god be my witness
I will restore my pride.*

Chapter 5

Dyslexia, Drama and Other Difficulties

Associated conditions

As dyslexia is a specific learning difficulty, there are often other learning difficulties that may overlap and have an impact on learning. In my opinion the two that would relate most to drama and dyslexia are dyspraxia and language difficulties. Dyspraxia because drama can involve a degree of movement and co-ordination, and language difficulties because of the speech element in many drama activities.

Dyspraxia

The following information has been provided by the Dyspraxia Foundation.

Dyspraxia and dyslexia overlap and often co-exist in the same person. Dyspraxia is an impairment of the organisation of movement and is often accompanied by problems with language, perception and thought. Dyslexia is primarily a difficulty with learning to read, write and spell and is often accompanied by other problems such as poor organisational skills. The pattern of difficulties experienced by a person with dyspraxia may vary widely, as with dyslexia.

There may also be overlaps with conditions such as ADD (Attention Deficit Disorder), ADHD (Attention Deficit Hyperactivity Disorder), Asperger's Syndrome and dyscalculia (difficulty with mathematical concepts). Some people with dyspraxia have tactile defensiveness – they are over-sensitive to touch. Others may have articulatory dyspraxia, which causes difficulties with speaking and pronunciation.

People with dyspraxia often suffer from low self-esteem. They may suffer from depression, have mental health problems and experience emotional and behavioural difficulties.

What is dyspraxia?

Developmental dyspraxia is an impairment or immaturity of the organisation of movement. It is an immaturity in the way that the brain processes information. This results in messages not being properly or fully transmitted. The term dyspraxia comes from the word 'praxis', which means 'doing, acting'. Dyspraxia affects the planning of what to do and how to do it; it is associated with problems of perception, language and thought.

Dyspraxia is thought to affect up to 10 per cent of the population and up to 2 per cent severely. Males are four times more likely to be affected than females. Dyspraxia sometimes runs in families and there may be an overlap with related conditions.

Other names for dyspraxia include Developmental Co-Ordination Disorder (DCD), Perceptuo-Motor Dysfunction and Motor Learning Difficulties. It used to be known as Minimal Brain Damage and Clumsy Child Syndrome.

Statistically, it is likely that there is one child with dypraxia in every class of 30 children. We need to make sure that everyone understands and knows how best to help this significant minority.

Reading and spelling

Children with dyspraxia may have difficulties with reading and spelling. Limited concentration, poor listening skills and literal use of language may have an effect on reading and spelling ability. A child may read well but not understand some of the concepts in the language. The child may also be reluctant to read because of articulation difficulties or because he/she lacks self-confidence.

Exercises may be beneficial for children with reading and spelling difficulties. Take Time *by Mary Nash-Wortham and Jean Hunt (1997) provides a series of exercises for parents, teachers and therapists that can be carried out with children. Computers can also help with reading and spelling:* Wordshark 2 *(NCTE 1999) is a widely used program, available from the Dyspraxia Foundation.*

45

Research has shown that children with developmental verbal dyspraxia whose speech difficulties persist beyond the age of 5.6 years are at risk of having literacy difficulties. The risk is increased if there is a family history of speech, language or specific learning difficulties.

The child with developmental verbal dyspraxia has an impaired speech processing system which affects their ability to make sound–letter links and to carry out phonological awareness tasks (e.g. segmenting, blending, rhyming etc.) essential for literacy acquisition. Spelling is usually more affected than reading.

Dyspraxia in children

Although dyspraxia may be diagnosed at any stage, increasing numbers of children are identified as having the condition. Early recognition of dyspraxia will enable early intervention and practical steps to help a child achieve his/her potential. Children whose dyspraxia is identified at an early stage are less likely to have problems with acceptance by their peers and with lowered self-esteem.

When children become teenagers their problems may change, as social and organisational difficulties become more pressing.

The Dyspraxia Foundation can help and support you and your child through its services and publications.

Symptoms

3 years old

Symptoms are evident from an early age. Babies are usually irritable from birth and may exhibit significant feeding problems. They are slow to achieve expected developmental milestones. For example, by the age of eight months they still may not sit independently.

Many children with dyspraxia fail to go through the crawling stages, preferring to 'bottom shuffle' and then walk. They usually avoid tasks which require good manual dexterity.

3 to 5 years old

Children with dyspraxia may demonstrate some of these types of behaviour:

- *very high levels of motor activity, including feet swinging and tapping when seated, hand-clapping or twisting; unable to stay still;*

- *high levels of excitability, with a loud/shrill voice;*
- *easily distressed and prone to temper tantrums;*
- *may constantly bump into objects and fall over;*
- *hands flap when running;*
- *difficulty with pedalling a tricycle or similar toy;*
- *lack of any sense of danger (jumping from heights etc.);*
- *messy eating – they may prefer to eat with fingers and may frequently spill drinks;*
- *avoidance of constructional toys, such as jigsaws or building blocks;*
- *poor fine motor skills; difficulty in holding a pencil or using scissors; drawings may appear immature;*
- *lack of imaginative play – may show little interest in 'dressing up' or in playing appropriately in a home corner or Wendy house;*
- *limited creative play;*
- *isolation within the peer group – rejected by peers they may prefer adult company;*
- *laterality (left- or right-handedness) still not established;*
- *persistent language difficulties;*
- *sensitive to sensory stimulation, including high levels of noise, tactile defensiveness, wearing new clothes;*
- *limited response to verbal instruction – may be slow to respond and may have problems with comprehension;*
- *limited concentration – tasks often left unfinished.*

If dyspraxia is not identified, problems can persist and affect the child at school. Increasing frustration and lowering of self-esteem can result.

7 years old
Problems may include:
- *difficulties in adapting to structured school routine;*
- *difficulties in PE lessons;*
- *slow at dressing; unable to tie shoelaces;*
- *barely legible handwriting;*
- *immature drawing and copying skills;*
- *limited concentration and poor listening skills;*
- *literal use of language;*
- *inability to remember more than two or three instructions at once;*
- *slow completion of class work;*

- *continued high levels of motor activity;*
- *hand flapping or clapping when excited;*
- *tendency to become easily distressed and emotional;*
- *problems with co-ordinating a knife and fork;*
- *inability to form relationships with other children;*
- *sleeping difficulties, including wakefulness at night and nightmares;*
- *reporting of physical symptoms, such as migraine, headaches, feeling sick.*

8 to 9 years (Primary education)
Children with dyspraxia may have become disaffected with the education system. Handwriting is often a particular difficulty. By the time they reach secondary school their attendance record is often poor.

Dyspraxia in teenagers
Life as a teenager can be particularly difficult if you have dyspraxia. All teenagers have to cope with bodily and emotional changes. Those with dyspraxia may find that their co-ordination and ability to cope with daily life is affected by those changes.

School or college may become particularly challenging, academically and socially. Examinations can be the cause of stress and uncertainty.

Teenagers are particularly aware of appearing different and may be acutely self-conscious about their appearance. The Dyspraxia Foundation's newsletter for teenagers, *Dyspraxia.net*, is a forum for teenagers with dyspraxia to share their problems.

Specific language impairment
It must be noted that the link between Specific Language Impairment and Specific Language Difficulties is well documented (Stackhouse and Wells 1991) and that levels of expressive and receptive syntax and semantics in the pre-reading years influence later reading and spelling ability.

Language is an important communication tool as well as being a powerful cognitive one; it aids thinking, memory and learning. The consequences of SLI may not just be restricted to communication; it covers all areas of language difficulties, from the actual muscles used for speech production to the ability to use and understand language at all. Specific Language Impairment can have other names such as 'language delay' or 'developmental dyslexia'.

Areas of difficulty can include: speech apparatus; phonology; grammar; semantics; pragmatics; and prosody.

If results are to be achieved, extra help, i.e. from a speech therapist, should be introduced as early as possible. As for dyslexia, it is important to understand that each person is an individual and that intervention strategies work differently for different people. Someone who needs the long-term help of a speech therapist will often be statemented with special educational needs. There are some important factors to be considered with specific language impairment. These are shown below:

- late talking in childhood may be a sign of SLI;
- a child with SLI does not necessarily have a low IQ or poor learning ability;
- speech impediments are different for language disorders;
- an incomplete understanding of verbs is an indicator of SLI;
- reading and learning will be affected by SLI;
- SLI can be diagnosed precisely and accurately;
- the condition may be genetic;
- the nature of the disability limits a child's exposure to language;
- early intervention can begin during pre-school.

Apraxia of speech

(The following information has been provided by the Dyspraxia Foundation.)

Children with developmental verbal dyspraxia have difficulty in making and co-ordinating the precise movements required for the production of clear speech, and yet there is no evidence of damage to nerves or muscles. They have difficulty in producing individual speech sounds and in sequencing sounds together in words. As a result, their speech is often unintelligible even to family members.

The speech disorder is the predominant presentation but children with developmental verbal dyspraxia may also have oro-motor dyspraxia – affecting their ability to make and co-ordinate the movements of the larynx, lips, tongue, and palate – and/or generalised dyspraxia, affecting gross and fine body movements. The favoured term in the UK is developmental verbal dyspraxia. However, it is also sometimes referred to as articulatory dyspraxia, and in the USA the usual term is developmental or childhood apraxia of speech.

Speech and language therapists usually diagnose developmental verbal dyspraxia by referring to checklists of characteristics and identifying a symptom cluster of presenting features. In addition to speech characteristics, checklists usually refer to commonly reported language, learning, clinical and motor characteristics.

Characteristics identified in the literature include:

- *speech characteristics;*
- *a limited range of consonant and vowel speech sounds;*
- *overuse of some sounds (favourite articulation);*
- *vowel distortions;*
- *inconsistent production;*
- *breakdown in sequencing in words, particularly as length increases;*
- *errors of omission and substitution – idiosyncratic substitutions may occur;*
- *glottal stop insertions and substitutions;*
- *voice difficulties affecting volume, length, pitch and quality;*
- *resonance difficulties affecting the overall tone of the speech;*
- *prosodic difficulties affecting rate, rhythm, stress, intonation;*
- *unintelligible speech;*
- *co-occurring characteristics;*
- *family history of speech, language or literacy difficulties;*
- *delayed language development – expressive usually more affected than receptive;*
- *delayed development of early speech skills, e.g. babbling;*
- *feeding difficulties;*
- *oral dyspraxia affecting movements of the larynx, lips, tongue or palate;*
- *generalised developmental dyspraxia affecting fine and/or gross motor co-ordination;*
- *literacy difficulties affecting reading, spelling and writing.*

Intervention and progress

Developmental verbal dyspraxia has been described as an unfolding and changing condition. The range of problems experienced 'unfold' as the child progresses and more demands are placed on him/her. As a result, the presentation of a child with developmental verbal dyspraxia is different according to age and stage of development. Unfortunately, this complicates diagnosis.

Help for children with developmental verbal dyspraxia

Children with speech difficulties should be referred to a speech and language therapist as early as possible. This can be arranged through a GP or Health Visitor or by contacting your local clinic or health centre. The speech and language therapist will be able to assess your child, identify the presenting difficulties and advise on management. He/she will be able to advise whether a label of developmental verbal dyspraxia is appropriate to describe your child's speech difficulties or whether another descriptor is more appropriate. Diagnosis of developmental verbal dyspraxia is complex and often becomes clearer over time.

Your therapist may also prefer to describe your child's difficulties rather than assign a label; e.g. 'Tom has a severe speech disorder, characterised by typical dyspraxic features', rather than 'Tom has developmental verbal dyspraxia'. This is accepted practice within the speech and language therapy profession.

It is generally recognised that children with developmental verbal dyspraxia do not get better without help. Usually they require regular, direct therapy delivered by a speech and language therapist, supported by frequent practice outside the therapy sessions at home and/or in school.

The Nuffield Dyspraxia Programme (1985,1992 and forthcoming) is one of the only published therapy approaches specifically for developmental verbal dyspraxia and is used widely by speech and language therapists in the UK and overseas. It offers a systematic approach to the assessment and treatment of developmental verbal dyspraxia and is particularly suitable for children aged 3–7.

In the early stages of the Nuffield Dyspraxia Programme, basic oro-motor exercises are advised to help the child develop with accurate and rapid movements of all areas of the speech apparatus in preparation for co-ordinating these movements in the production of speech sounds. If you are waiting to see a speech and language therapist, or you want to start doing something helpful with your child, these exercises provide a good starting point.

Summary

This chapter has provided some insights into other related conditions that can be associated with dyslexia. The examples used of dyspraxia and specific language impairment are particularly relevant to drama. This underlines the view that every child has to have their individual needs identified and catered for within the curriculum.

Chapter 6

Parents and Dyslexia

This book can be accessed by parents as well as teachers. It is therefore beneficial to incorporate the responses of parents of dyslexic children. It is also important that teachers are aware of parents' views. Dyslexic children have needs but so do the family. It is important to be able to handle day-to-day activities and to understand how you can help your child.

This chapter is based upon the work of Pat Heaton who collected parent responses from a questionnaire.

On being told that their child is dyslexic many parents feel relief. It will have been frustrating to know that there was a problem with their child but not knowing what the problem was, and it can be a relief to finally put a name to the problem. Explanations of learning failures can range from brain tumours to being mentally retarded, and parents are vulnerable in that they often do not know what to believe. It is common for parents to feel angry and guilty – angry for not getting help sooner and guilty for forcing learning or for being dyslexic themselves. The psychologist's report on a child will also reveal the emotional and behavioural aspects of dyslexia and can often bring families closer once they start discussing the situation, instead of blaming one another. On the other hand, some parents prefer to keep the diagnosis to themselves, thus avoiding other people's opinions. Sometimes, naivety to the condition may result in a negative attitude to the student.

The questionnaire discussed labelling, its advantages being that those with a knowledge of dyslexia will be empathetic, but disadvantages may occur in later life where, for example, an employer might reject a dyslexic candidate in favour of a 'more intelligent' one. Heaton says that 'It is important to remember that recognition is only a step along the way, so to speak.' The disability causes many problems, some more obvious than others. Assessment and diagnosis merely identify the disability; they do not cure it.

Once a child is recognised as being dyslexic, provision can be made to help with education. More support can be offered at school but that can take time. Some parents may opt for outside private tuition, but this can be a strain, both financially, for the parents, and for the student, who already has to work harder at school to maintain a decent level of learning and attainment. This pressure can begin to affect everyday family life, causing irritability and shyness.

We must not forget that dyslexia is not just restricted to reading and writing; memory and organisational skills can also be a problem. Parents can help their child by marking or coding days on a big calendar, e.g. green = PE, geography and history – then perhaps put green stickers on the appropriate books and bags. Organisation and awareness is central to coping with dyslexia. Prepare in advance for important meetings and events. Meet with other parents of dyslexic students. Some parents find that enrolling on a learning difficulties course can help them to understand their child's condition.

Parents' hurdles

Gavin Reid (Reid 2004) asked parents for their views on the difficulties they experienced having a child with dyslexia. The questions he asked included the following:

- What are the factors that made it difficult for you as a parent of a child with dyslexia?
- From where did you get your support?
- What strategies did you, as a parent, use to help support your child?

The responses to these questions were very illuminating. One of the parents found that the main challenges in parenting a child with dyslexia included:

- helping to maintain the child's self-esteem;
- helping the child start new work when he/she had not consolidated previous work;

- protecting the dignity of the child when dealing with professionals/ therapists;
- personal organisation of the child;
- peer insensitivity; and
- misconceptions about dyslexia.

This response is quite interesting because it touches on some of the key aspects, particularly the emotional ones, of dyslexia. It also touches on the misunderstandings and misconceptions that many people can have about the condition.

This parent also provided additional information and suggested that:

> self-esteem is a huge issue and one that is not helped by dyslexia being seen as a deficit! The continued emphasis on academic achievement and the issues of labelling are problematic for me. A major difficulty with the teaching profession is attitudinal – a lack of knowledge on dyslexia is apparent –although I have found there are also some exceptional teachers, but it is always difficult for a parent to know what advice to take. By the time they are in a position to decide, it can be too late, or less effective than it could have been.
>
> The balance between home and school is a key issue, and although I have had little advice on this I have still had to argue a case for the need for school to understand the fatigue element in a long day. I feel like my child is a square peg in a round hole. (Reid 2004)

Secondary school

Once in secondary school it is important that every member of staff involved with the student is aware of the child's particular difficulties. It is important to keep the school updated about any external meetings or appointments so that the teaching staff can plan ahead.

As mentioned before, memory can cause problems for the dyslexic student and this can be infuriating for all concerned. Some parents find that a calculator is best for times tables work in order not to have to go over the same calculations every day. Stories can be another coping device, as can post-it notes around the house. When I was studying I found this useful and would write or put important pictures on papers around the house on objects I would spend some amount of time looking at – for example, on a cereal box, when having my breakfast, or the bathroom mirror, when I was doing my hair.

The use of information technology at home can be important, not only to run a spellcheck but also to aid with presentation of work, something that some dyslexic students struggle with.

For parents there is no easy way of dealing with dyslexia. What works for one family may not work for another. It is all about trial and error and, above all, patience. This is clear from the words of one parent who responded to the questionnaire in Gavin Reid's research:

> Remember to take time out. Have fun as a family. Home is a safe place – no criticism. Try not to push, push, push. Encourage your child to pursue the things he/she is good at. Keep self-esteem high. Set up good working relationships with the school teacher. Keep trying; there is help available; just keep chipping away. (Reid 2004)

Summary for parents

- Find out what the school will do to help your child.
- If it is possible, it may be helpful to fund an external dyslexia tutor who can help.
- Remember that your child is intelligent and that it is no-one's fault that he/she is dyslexic – do not blame yourself.
- Colour-coding books and materials, as well as days on the calendar, can help.
- Organisation and awareness are the control to success.
- Meet with other parents of dyslexic children; you are not on your own.

Be patient!

References and Further Reading

Bradley, L. and Bryant, P. (1991) 'Phonological skills before and after learning to read', in Brady, S.A. and Shankweiler, D.P. (eds) *Phonological Processes in Literacy*. London: Lawrence Erlbaum.

Campbell, D. (2001) 'The Mozart Effect: Tapping the Power of Music to Heal the Body, Strengthen the Mind and Unlock the Creative Spirit'. London: Hodder and Stoughton.

Department for Education (1994) *The Code of Practice for the Identification and Assessment of Special Educational Needs*. London: DfE.

Department for Education and Employment (1998) *Framework for Teaching the National Literacy Strategy*. London: DfEE.

Department for Education and Employment (2000) *Draft Revised SEN Code of Practice*. London: DfEE.

Department for Education and Skills (2001) *Special Educational Needs Code of Practice*. London: DfES.

Dunn, R., Krimsky, J., Murray, J. and Quinn, P. (1985) 'Light up their lives: a review of research on the effects of lighting on children's achievement'. *The Reading Teacher*, **38** (9), 863-9.

Fawcett, A.J. (2002) 'Dyslexia and literacy: key issues for research', in G. Reid and J. Wearmouth *Dyslexia and Literacy: Theory and Practice*. Chichester: Wiley.

Fawcett, A.J. and Nicolson, R.I. (1996) *The Dyslexia Screening Test*. London: The Psychological Corporation.

Frith, U. (1995) 'Dyslexia: can we have a shared theoretical framework?' *Educational and Child Psychology*, **12** (1), 6-17.

Frith, U. (2002) 'Resolving the paradoxes of Dyslexia', in G. Reid and J. Wearmouth *Dyslexia and Literacy: Theory and Practice*. Chichester: Wiley.

Galaburda, A. (ed.) (1993) *Dyslexia and Development: Neurobiological Aspects of Extraordinary Brains*. Cambridge, MA: Harvard University Press.

Given, B.K. and Reid, G. (1999) *Learning Styles: A Guide for Teachers and Parents*. St Annes on Sea: Red Rose Publications.

Hatcher, J. and Snowling, M.J. (2002) 'The phonological representations hypothesis of dyslexia: from theory to practice', in G. Reid and J. Wearmouth *Dyslexia and Literacy: Theory and Practice.* Chichester: Wiley.

JCQ (2001) *Regulations and Guidance,* London: Joint Council for Qualifications.

Leonard, L.B. (1998) *Children with Specific Language Impairment.* Cambridge, MA: MIT Press.

Morton, J. and Frith, U. (1993) 'What lessons for dyslexia from Down Syndrome?' Comments on Cossu, Rossini and Marshall, *Cognition,* **48**, 289-96.

Morton, J. and Frith, U. (1995) 'Causal modelling: a structured approach to developmental psychopathology', in D. Cicchetti and D.J. Cohen (eds) *Manual of Developmental Psychopathology.* New York: Wiley, pp. 357-90.

Mutter, V., Hulme, C. and Snowling, M.J. (1997) *Phonological Abilities Test.* San Francisco, CA: The Psychological Corporation.

Nash-Wortham, M. and Hunt, J. (1997) *Take Time: Movement Exercises for Parents, Teachers and Therapists of Children with Difficulties in Speaking, Reading, Writing and Spelling.*(4th edn). Stourbridge: The Robinswood Press.

NCTE (National Centre for Technology in Education) (1999) *Wordshark 2.* London: White Space.

Nicolson, R.I. (1996) 'Developmental dyslexia: past, present and future'. *Dyslexia,* **2** (3), 190-207.

Nicolson, R.I. and Fawcett, A.J. (1999) 'Developmental dyslexia: the role of the cerebellum'. *Dyslexia: An International Journal of Research and Practice,* 5 155-77.

Nicolson, R.I. and Siegel, L. (1996) Special issue on Dyslexia and Intelligence (Editor's Foreword). *Dyslexia,* **2** (3), 153.

Nuffield Centre for Speech and Language Therapy (1985, 1992, forthcoming) *The Nuffield Centre Dyspraxia Programme.* Available from Nuffield Hearing and Speech Centre, RNTNE Division of Royal Free Hampstead NHS Trust, Gray's Inn Road, London WC1X 8DA, tel. 020 7915 1535.

Peer, L. (2001) 'Dyslexia and its manifestations in the secondary school', in L. Peer and G. Reid (eds) *Dyslexia: Successful Inclusion in the Secondary School.* London: David Fulton.

Reid, G. (2003) *Dyslexia: A Practitioner's Handbook* (3rd edn). Chichester: Wiley.

Reid, G. (2004) *Dyslexia: A Complete Guide for Parents.* Chichester: Wiley.

Reid, G. and Given, B.K. (1999) 'The interactive observation style identification', in B.K. Given and G. Reid, *Learning Styles: A Guide for Teachers and Parents.* St Annes on Sea: Red Rose Publications.

Rice, M.L. (2000) 'Grammatical symptoms of specific language impairment', in D.V.M. Bishop and L.B. Leonard (eds) *Speech and Language Impairment in Children: Causes, Characteristics, Intervention and Outcomes.* Hove: Psychology Press, pp.17-34.

Rice, M.L. (2002) 'A unified model of specific and general language delay: grammatical tense as a clinical marker of unexpected variation', in Y. Levy and J. Schaeffer (eds) *Language Competence Across Populations: Towards a Definition of Specific Language Impairment.* Mahwah, NJ: Lawrence Erlbaum, pp. 63-95.

Rice, M.L. and Wilcox, K. (eds) (1995) *Building a Language-Focused Curriculum for the Preschool Classroom: A Foundation for Life-long Communication.* Baltimore, ML: Brookes Publishing Company.

Schuele, C.M. and Hadley, P. (1999) 'Potential advantages of introducing specific language impairment to families'. *American Journal of Speech–Language Pathology*, **8**, 11-22.

Snowling, M.J. (1998) 'Dyslexia as a phonological deficit: evidence and implications'. *Child Psychology and Psychiatry Review*, **1**, 4-11.

Snowling, M.J. (2000) *Dyslexia* (2nd edn). Oxford: Blackwell.

Special Educational Needs and Disability Act (SENDA) (2001). London: Her Majesty's Government.

Stackhouse, J. and Wells, B. (1991) 'Dyslexia: the obvious and hidden speech disorder', in M. Snowling and M. Thomson (eds) *Dyslexia: Integrating Theory and Practice*. London: Whurr.

Stanovich, K.E. (1991) 'Discrepancy definitions of reading disability: has intelligence led us astray? *Reading Research Quarterly*, **36**, 7-29.

Stanovich, K.E. (1994) 'Annotation: does dyslexia exist?' *Journal of Child Psychology and Psychiatry*, **21**, 7-9.

Stanovich, K.E. (1996) 'Towards a more inclusive definition of dyslexia'. *Dyslexia*, **2** (3), 154-66.

Stanovich. K.E.(1998) 'Explaining the difference between the dyslexic and the garden variety poor readers: the phonological core model'. *Journal of Learning Disabilities*, **21** (10), 590-604.

Tager-Flusber, H. and Cooper, J. (1999) 'Present and future possibilities for defining a phenotype for specific language impairment'. *Journal of Speech, Language and Hearing Research*, **42**, 1275-8.

Tomblin, J.B. (1997) 'Prevalence of SLI in kindergarten children'. *Journal of Speech, Language and Hearing Research*, **40**, 1245-60.

Tunmer, W.E. and Chapman, J. (1996) 'A developmental model of dyslexia: Can the construct be saved?' *Dyslexia*, **2** (3), 179-89.

West, T.G. (1991, 1997) *In the Mind's Eye*. New York: Prometheus.

Wolf, M. and O'Brien, B. (2001) 'On issues of time, fluency and intervention', in A. Fawcett (ed.) *Dyslexia, Theory and Good Practice*. London: Whurr.

Index

access
  to curriculum 20
  to texts 19
activities *see* games
advertising campaigns 34
alienation 41–2
annotated texts 19, 20
assessment 13, 14
  barriers and 15, 16
  by mind-mapping 5
  by recording 4
  by reporting 16
  by writing frames 4–5
attainment 3, 38, 39–41, 42
automaticity 7–8

barriers 15, 16
behaviour 39–40
breathing techniques 4
bullying 39, 40, 41, 42
Buzan, T. 22

Campbell, D. 23
cerebellar deficit hypothesis 6
Chapman, J. 8–9
children vii, 43 *see also individual terms*
colour 23
components, meaning and 9–10
computers 55
  mind-mapping by 22
confidence 2, 38, 39, 40, 41, 42
co-operation 34, 36–7
co-ordination 34, 35–6, 37
coursework 14, 18
  scope 16–17

creativity 12, 17, 34
cross-curricular skills 20, 21

DAD (Dyslexia Automaticity Deficit) 7–8
design skills 16–17
detail analysis 7
double-deficit hypothesis 7
drama 11, 41 *see also individual terms*
dyslexia 54–5
  characteristics 1–2
  conflicts in vii, 6
  defined 1, 8
  prevalence 1
  scope 1
  see also individual terms
Dyslexia Automaticity Deficit (DAD) 7–8
dyspraxia
  children's characteristics 46–8
  defined 45
  labels 45
  on language 45–6, 49–52
  overlaps with 44
  prevalence 45
  recognition 46, 47
  scope 44–5
  teenagers 48

educational psychologists 16
engagement 12, 18, 19, 20, 22
environment 22–3
exams 14
  annotated texts in 19, 20
  reviewing in 18–19
  scope 17–18, 20
  see also tests